G

CENGAGE Learning

Poetry for Students, Volume 12

Staff

Editors: Jennifer Smith and Elizabeth Thomason.

Contributing Editors: Anne Marie Hacht, Michael L. LaBlanc, Ira Mark Milne.

Managing Editor, Literature Content: Dwayne D. Hayes.

Managing Editor, Literature Product: David Galens.

Publisher, Literature Product: Mark Scott.

Research: Victoria B. Cariappa, *Research Manager*. Cheryl Warnock, *Research Specialist*. Tamara Nott, Tracie A. Richardson, *Research Associates*. Nicodemus Ford, Sarah Genik, Timothy Lehnerer, Ron Morelli, *Research Assistants*.

Permissions: Maria Franklin, *Permissions Manager*. Margaret Chamberlain, *Permissions Specialist*. Jacqueline Jones, *Permissions Assistant*.

Manufacturing: Mary Beth Trimper, *Manager, Composition and Electronic Prepress.* Evi Seoud, *Assistant Manager, Composition Purchasing and Electronic Prepress.* Stacy Melson, *Buyer.*

Imaging and Multimedia Content Team: Barbara Yarrow, *Manager.* Randy Bassett, *Imaging Supervisor.* Robert Duncan, Dan Newell, *Imaging Specialists.* Pamela A. Reed, *Imaging Coordinator.* Leitha Etheridge-Sims, Mary Grimes, David G. Oblender, *Image Catalogers.* Robyn V. Young, *Project Manager.* Dean Dauphinais, *Senior Image Editor.* Kelly A. Quin, *Image Editor.*

Product Design Team: Kenn Zorn, *Product Design Manager.* Pamela A. E. Galbreath, *Senior Art Director.* Michael Logusz, *Graphic Artist.*

the publisher will be corrected in future editions.

Copyright © 2001
The Gale Group
27500 Drake Rd.
Farmington Hills, MI 48331-3535

ISBN 0-7876-4690-3
ISSN 1094-7019

Printed in the United States of America.
10 9 8 7 6 5 4 3 2 1

The Rape of the Lock

Alexander Pope 1714

Introduction

"The Rape of the Lock," originally published as *The Rape of the Locke: An Heroi-Comical Poem* (1712), is a mock-epic based upon an actual disagreement between two aristocratic English families during the eighteenth century. Lord Petre (the Baron in the poem) surprises the beautiful Arabella Fermor (Belinda) by clipping off a lock of hair. At the suggestion of his friend and with Arabella Fermor's approval, Alexander Pope used imagination, hyperbole, wit, and gentle satire to inflate this trivial social slip-up into an earth-shaking catastrophe of cosmic consequence. The poem is generally described as one of Pope's most brilliant satires.

The poem makes serious demands upon the

reader, not only because of its length but also because it requires a background knowledge of epic literature and some understanding of the trappings of upperclass England. "The Rape of the Lock" constantly shifts between mocking silly social conventions of the aristocracy (such as elaborate courtship rituals) and satirizing serious literary conventions of traditional epic literature (such as its lofty style, exhaustive descriptions of warriors readying for battle, and heavy doses of mythology). With many allusions to Homer's *Iliad* and *Odyssey,* Virgil's *Aeneid,* and John Milton's *Paradise Lost,* the speaker compares the loss of Belinda's hair to the great battles of classic epic literature. The speaker describes Belinda applying makeup as if she were a warrior going to battle. While playing a game of cards, the Baron sneaks up behind Belinda and performs the "tragic" snipping of the lock of hair. An army of gnomes and sprites attempts to protect Belinda to no avail. Belinda demands the restoration of her lock and another "battle" ensues. Finally, the lock ascends skyward as a new star to beautify the heavens.

Pope was born on May 21, 1688, in London, England, the son of Alexander Pope, a London linen merchant, and his second wife, Edith Turner. Pope attended two Catholic academies before the family moved from London in 1700 to live in the village of Binfield. A new law, prohibiting Catholics from living within ten miles of the city of London, forced the family to move. The relocation to Binfield enabled Pope to make enduring friendships with other Catholic exiles like himself. Pope's early education was sporadic. He learned to read and write at home and was taught Latin and Greek by priests. By the age of twelve, he was already well versed in Greek, Roman, and English literature, and he diligently emulated the works of his favorite poets. At twelve, Pope contracted Pott's disease, a tuberculosis of the spine, from infected milk. The disease left him with a crooked spine and a severe weakness, which caused him almost continual headaches for the rest of his life.

Pope's first published work, "Pastorals," a group of lyric poems on rural themes, was published in 1709. Two years later, he published "An Essay on Criticism," a treatise on literary theory written in verse couplets. The impressiveness of this feat caught the attention of English literary society, and with the publication of the first two cantos of *The Rape of the Lock* in 1712 (expanded to five cantos in 1714) Pope was regarded as one of the most prominent poets of the age. He eventually became the first independently wealthy, full-time writer in English history.

Despite such success, Pope suffered throughout his career from recurring attacks against him for his Catholicism, his political sympathies, and his literary criticism, which often raised the anger of the authors he analyzed. Some of these attacks were personal, commenting unfavorably upon his physical appearance. Much of Pope's later satirical writings were aimed at those who had criticized him over the years. Pope's last years were spent revising the body of his writings in preparation for a complete, edited edition of his works. He died on May 30, 1744 of acute asthma and dropsy before the task was completed.

Poem Summary

Lines 1–6

The speaker, in typical epic fashion, invokes his muse to inspire him in his composition. Traditionally, the goddess presiding over epic poetry is Calliope. In this case, Pope's friend John Caryll is the "muse" who suggested the poet attempt a playful satire to cure the family squabble that erupted when Lord Petre cut a lock of hair from Miss Arabella Fermor. The speaker's aim is to raise this insignificant dispute to a "mighty contest."

Lines 7–12

In these three couplets, the speaker poses three questions the mock-epic will attempt to answer: why would a lord assault a gentle maiden?; why would an aristocratic lady reject a lord?; how can "mighty rage" hide in polite society?

Lines 13–26

The speaker uses personification, describing the sun as "Sol" who tries to awaken the poem's heroine, Belinda, and her lapdog, Shock. Pope uses the word "sylph" to mean an imaginary fairy—a creature that inhabits the air.

Lines 27–66

Ariel's speech takes up most of Canto I, continuing to line 114. The speaker introduces an army of supernatural, imaginary creatures because it is one of the conventions of epic poetry being satirized. Homer, Virgil, and Milton made use of classical mythology to puff up the significance of their heroes' exploits. Pope uses characters from Rosicrucian mythology such as Ariel (Canto I), Umbriel (Canto IV), and Thalestris (Canto V). According to Rosicrucian myth and the theories of metaphysical philosopher Paracelsus, all things were believed to have been made of four Aristotelian elements: fire, water, earth, and air. In lines 59–66, the speaker mentions all four elements and the supernatural creatures associated with them: salamanders (fire); nymphs (water); gnomes (earth); and sylphs (air). The intent of this section is to elaborate on the background of the mythological creatures that come and go throughout the course of "The Rape of the Lock." The mythology contributes weight and gravity to an otherwise light social satire. The speaker satirizes the conventions of epic poetry and literary tradition as well as the social vanity of the aristocratic Belinda.

Media Adaptations

- A recording of "The Rape of the Lock" is included in the two-cassette set, *Penguin English Verse: The Eighteenth Century: Swift to Crabbe, Volume 3.* The tapes were released in 1996 by Penguin Highbridge Audio.

Lines 67–114

Ariel tells Belinda that sylphs embrace all the fair and chaste maidens of society by assuming any shape they want, an allusion to Milton's description of the army of devils in *Paradise Lost.* Ariel issues the vague warning of "some dread event" impending upon her before the day is out, but he does not specify what this dread event may be. Ariel concludes his long speech by saying that Belinda should above all "beware of men," a hint that the impending doom relates to her flirtations with men. Line 101, "where wigs with wigs, with sword-knots sword-knots strive" is an allusion to Homer's *Iliad* and his description of the Greek forces readying their weapons to battle the Trojans. Also in this speech, Ariel resembles the angel Raphael, the angel who came to Eve in the Garden of Eden to warn her of Satan's approach, in Milton's *Paradise Lost.*

Lines 115–120

Shock, Belinda's lapdog, thinks that his mistress has slept too long and licks Belinda with his tongue. As Belinda pulls herself out of bed, she sees a "billet-deux" or love-letter on her bed. Reading the charming words of some admirer, Belinda's "vision" or lesson from Ariel disappears from her memory. Belinda forgets Ariel's warning about the need to beware of jealousy, vanity, pride, and impertinent men.

Lines 121–148

Belinda goes to her toilet or cosmetic table to prepare herself for the day to be spent in fashionable society. With the help of her servant Betty, whom the speaker describes as "the inferior priestess," Belinda grooms herself and accumulates intense pride in her beauty. This masterfully written section catalogues the exotic jewelry, pins, powders, perfumes, mirrors, tortoise shell and ivory combs, blushes, and rouges that Belinda uses to heighten her exquisite beauty and egoistic sense of importance. The speaker says in line 139 that "Now awful Beauty puts on all its arms," meaning "awful" as "aweinspiring" the way the enemy watches the epic hero prepare his battle gear for combat and is awestruck at his weaponry and prowess. Also, the speaker presents Belinda at the "altar" of her beauty as a religious analogy, satirizing Belinda as the high priestess of vanity. The speaker also uses the catalogue of beauty aids as an allusion to the serious epic convention of describing soldiers readying for battle. Thus, Belinda "arms" herself for "battle" with the Baron, about whom Ariel has indirectly warned her.

Lines 149–166

Like many chapters of the *Iliad* or the *Odyssey,* Canto II begins with the sun rising over "the purple main," or sea reddened by dawn to a royal purple. Belinda is presented as the sun's rival because her self-appointed radiance shines as she drifts in a boat upon the river Thames. Surrounded by well-dressed admirers and nymphs, Belinda sails from London to Hampton Court, the royal palace about fifteen miles up the river. Belinda extends her smile to all surrounding courtiers like a true coquette. The speaker says that one look at Belinda's beautiful face would make anyone forget her female faults, if any were to be found.

Lines 167–182

The speaker mentions Belinda's two locks of hair that gracefully hang behind her in "sparkling ringlets," using similes to compare the locks with a labyrinth that enslaves admirers to her love or snares that trap the unsuspecting courtier dazzled by her beauty. The first mention of the Baron comes in line 177 as he admires the radiant locks and resolves to possess one by any fraudulent or deceptive means. So captivated by the beautiful Belinda, the Baron must possess her beauty somehow.

Lines 183–194

The speaker writes that before the sun rose, the Baron had built an altar to the goddess Love and arranged around it all his symbols of success with former mistresses: twelve French romances bound in gold, garters, gloves, "trophies," and love letters. The Baron had thrown himself prostrate before this Love altar, a parallel to Belinda's cosmetic altar, and prayed for powers from the goddess that would allow him to capture the lock and keep it forever. However, Love grants the Baron only half of his prayer that he might acquire the lock but not keep it forever. This line (193) foreshadows the conclusion of the poem.

Lines 195–220

All the sailing company enjoys the leisurely cruise upon the Thames river except the sylph Ariel, who is oppressed with gloom because his warning against vanity was lost upon Belinda. Line 199 demonstrates Pope's use of onomatopoeia because the sound of the words mimics the sense of the gentle ride upon the water. Ariel summons his army of sprites and sylphs—inhabitants of the air whose fluid bodies disappear in transparent forms. Ariel stands tall before the other sylphs just as the typical epic hero—Odysseus, Achilles, or Agamemnon—towers before the troops addressing them before combat.

Lines 221–290

The second long speech by Ariel concludes Canto II. Ariel reminds the sylph army that their humble purpose is to guard the fair maiden Belinda, protecting her beauty from harsh winds and brightening her complexion when she needs it. The impending threat approaches, says Ariel, the "black day" of some dire disaster or threat to Belinda's chastity and beauty. Therefore, special assignments are dealt out by Ariel. Ariel shows special care in assigning duties associated with the sylph's name: Zephyretta (the west wind) protects Belinda's fan; Brilliante protects the diamond earrings; Momentilla protects the watch; Crispissa (a word for curling) protects Belinda's favorite lock of hair. Ariel himself will guard Shock, the lapdog. Fifty sylphs are chosen to guard Belinda's petticoat, associated with her virginity. Though the petticoat is armed with stiff hoops and stout whale rib, danger is still possible, and so the sylphs are needed. Ariel concludes his speech admonishing that any sylph who neglects his watch "shall feel sharp vengeance" and severe physical punishment —like Ixion, who in Greek mythology was punished in the underworld by being bound to an ever-turning wheel. After Ariel's pep talk, the sylphs disperse to their assigned guardian posts, waiting anxiously for the disaster that beats down quickly upon them.

Lines 291–308

Belinda's boat approaches Hampton Court, a royal palace where the Baron lies in wait. Hampton Court is one home of Queen Ann of England. With Britain's noble statesmen, Queen Ann plots the fall of foreign tyrants and then engages in trivial social bantering at teatime. Belinda and her retinue of servants, admirers, and unseen sylphs enter the social scene of the court. Belinda is very much aware that her social reputation depends on how she might hold her fan or chit-chat with nobles and dignitaries.

Lines 309–334

In the afternoon, Belinda desires to play "ombre," a Spanish card game resembling whist or bridge, against two suitors, the Baron and a young man. The speaker describes each card in elaborate detail, its ranking suit and number, along with the invisible sylphs who guard each card. This resembles armies assembling for combat in epic poems such as the *Iliad.* Pope has carefully arranged the cards exactly according to the rules of ombre. The game is played with forty cards, the 10s, 9s, and 8s removed from play. Each player holds nine cards and Belinda's cards are winning at first. Ariel is perched upon a "Matadore," the highest trump cards. The trump cards are the ace of spades (Spadillio), the two of spades (Manillio), and the ace of clubs (Basto). The descending order of kings, queens, and jacks are described as readied for "the velvet plain" (or card table) a term used for the battlefield in epic poetry.

Lines 335–390

In this section, the actual game of ombre is described in astonishing detail. While Belinda is winning at first, the tide of "battle" turns in line 356 when the Baron sends his "warlike amazon" or Queen of spades to win the first of four tricks. The Baron's egoistic pride shows through as he wins the card game/battle. When the "routed army" begins to run away in line 371, confusion sets in. The speaker uses a parody of an epic simile in lines 371–376 to compare the losing cards with a confused army retreating from battle.

Lines 391–414

The speaker foreshadows "the fall" of Belinda's lock of hair in elevated language, comparing it to the fall of Eve in *Paradise Lost.* After the card game is finished and the Baron relishes his victory, coffee is served to the guests. Another convention of epic poetry is parodied, the epic repast or feast wherein warriors refresh themselves after battle or during a long journey. The speaker luxuriates in the lavish detail of the coffee beans, silver pots, lacquered tables, and delicate chinaware of the "feast." However, the strong smell of the coffee travels to the Baron's brain and inspires him to new stratagems to get the lock of hair. The speaker compares the Baron to Scylla in Greek mythology, the daughter of Nisus who was punished and turned into a sea bird because she cut from her father's head the purple lock upon which his safety depended.

Lines 415–436

Suddenly, Clarissa, one of the Baron's assistants—and also the heroine of a famous novel by Samuel Richardson—draws a pair of scissors out of her case. The speaker compares this action with the knight who is presented a battle-axe before a joust. Just as Belinda bends over to smell the fragrant aroma of coffee, a thousand sylphs rush over to guard her hair. They attempt in vain to warn Belinda by blowing back her hair and twitching her earrings. Ariel himself tries to enter into Belinda's thoughts to warn her, but he gives up in vain, resigned to the disastrous fate.

Lines 437–468

The "fatal engine" or the scissors held by the

Baron draw close to Belinda's lock; at the last moment, a sylph interposes and gets cut into two. Pope's use of phrases like "fatal engine" for scissors (line 439) or "the finney prey" for fish (line 174) are examples of poetic diction, a highly refined system of words used for exaggeration here but used seriously by lesser eighteenth-century poets. Poetic diction was criticized by later generations of poets and critics who felt that words elevated too far beyond their common usage distorted their meaning. While the sylph's parts can soon come together because he is made of a magical airy substance, as the scissors close, the lock is permanently severed from Belinda's head. Belinda screams as the lock falls into the Baron's hands. The Baron yells "the glorious prize is mine" and praises the scissors, comparing them with the Greek swords that brought down the walled fortress-city of Troy in the *Iliad*. The Baron yells that his honor, name, and praise will live forever because of his great conquering act of snipping the lock of hair— much like Odysseus did as he was leaving the cave of Polyphemus, the Cyclops in the *Odyssey*.

Lines 469–484

Ariel, the guardian sylph, cries bitterly and flies away. Because of the loss of her lock, Belinda feels more rage, resentment, and despair than all the scorned kings, virgins, and lovers of history— according to the speaker in his typically hyperbolic fashion. A melancholy gnome named Umbriel, whose name suggests shade or darkness, travels to the cave of Spleen. This is a digression or sub-plot and not a part of the main action of the poem. Queen Spleen is the Queen of all bad tempers, ill-nature, affectation, and every negative human quality. This section focusing on Umbriel's journey is a parody of the journey to the underworld that takes place in traditional epics such as Odyssey, *Aeneid,* and *Paradise Lost.*

Lines 485–546

The gnome Umbriel travels through the gloomy recesses of the underworld into the cave sheltered from all sunlight and air. Once Umbriel approaches the throne of Spleen, he notices the Queen's attendants and the languid, sickly atmosphere surrounding the place. Strange specters, phantoms, and snakes arise from the ground. The cave surely seems to be the pits of Hell. Umbriel begins his speech to Spleen in line 525, singing her praises because of her powers. Spleen rules over women with her "vapors" of hypochondria, melancholy, and peevishness. These were actual diagnoses used to describe the maladies of fashionable ladies of Pope's day. Spleen makes women act with inappropriately bad social manners. Umbriel says that Belinda has disdained Spleen's powers on earth because of Belinda's beauty and happiness. Umbriel asks Spleen for some power to touch Belinda with ill humor because if Belinda suffers, half the world will suffer with her (another of many wild exaggerations).

Lines 547–556

The cave goddess Spleen grants the request of Umbriel, giving him a bag filled with terrifying noises such as those expressed by female lungs: sighs, sobs, passions, and complaints typically associated with disappointment in love. This is an allusion to Homer's *Odyssey,* in which Odysseus gets a bag of winds from Aeolus, the god of wind, in order to propel his ship. In a vial, Spleen places fainting fears, sorrows, griefs, and flowing tears. The gnome rejoices and his black wings carry him away, back to earth.

Lines 557–588

Umbriel travels back to earth and finds Belinda in Thalestris' arms. Thalestris, another character from Rosicrucian mythology, is Queen of the Amazons, who are fierce and warlike women. Umbriel pours over Belinda's head the bag of noxious noises given to him by Spleen. Thalestris magnifies Belinda's suffering by chastising her, blaming her "rape" or loss of the lock of hair upon her carelessness; Ariel had attempted to warn Belinda in Canto I about such a catastrophe. Thalestris asks what good the elaborate beauty preparation did when Belinda fell prey to the Baron's scissors? Thalestris complains that fashionable ladies and gentlemen are talking behind Belinda's back about the rape and Belinda's loss of reputation. For someone who so values the pleasantries of social discourse amongst the upper crust, this is a fate worse than death. Meanwhile, the Baron gazes upon his "inestimable prize" of the lock of hair as it is encased in a ring upon his hand. All of Belinda's honor appears to be lost.

Lines 589–608

Thalestris goes to her brother, Sir Plume, and requests that he go to the Baron and demand the return of the lock of Belinda's hair. Sir Plume curses against the loss of the lock and considers the whole episode a worthless waste of time. However, Sir Plume honors Thalestris' request by going to the Baron. The Baron refuses to return his precious prize as long as he lives because he feels he won it for himself. The Baron wants to wear the ring with the lock of hair forever—against the prophecy given by the goddess Love in Canto II.

Lines 609–644

In these lines, Umbriel breaks the vial of sorrows, tears, and griefs over Belinda's head as she continues her intolerable suffering. Canto IV concludes with a long speech of lament by Belinda, in which she cries for the return of happy times. Belinda expresses regret that she ever came to Hampton Court and played ombre with the Baron. Belinda wishes that she had led a simple country life instead of entering into the dangerous affairs of polite society. If Belinda had kept her beauty concealed, she feels that she never would have suffered. Belinda would have dutifully uttered her prayers at home. In line 633, Belinda finally recalls the speech of Ariel, her guardian sylph who had warned her of the disaster. But Belinda did not listen at the time. Now, the other lock of hair sits "uncouth, alone" upon Belinda's head as she suffers in vain. If only she had listened to Ariel!

Lines 645–678

Thalestris' attempt to retrieve the lock through Sir Plume has failed. Clarissa, who had given the Baron the pair of scissors, speculates in a long speech about the vanity of women and the stupidity of the men who court them. All the luxuries of the rich are wasted upon this idle game of courtship, says Clarissa, since beauty must fade with age. These superficial attributes of beauty and charm pale in comparison with lasting qualities. The speech is summarized in the couplet in lines 677–678: "Beauties in vain their pretty eyes may roll; / Charms strike the sight, but merit wins the soul." Clarissa's speech is a parody of a speech given by the Greek warrior Sarpedon to Glaucus in Homer's *Iliad*. Alexander Pope knew the *Iliad* and *Odyssey* so well because he had translated both of them from Greek into English. Today, Pope's translations are still highly regarded.

Lines 679–700

Belinda frowns after Clarissa's speech. Thalestris calls Clarissa a prude for her moralizing tone. Thalestris gets ready an army of sylphs for another epic battle, the concluding action of the poem. Umbriel, sitting on a candlestick holder mounted on the wall, delights at the prospect of another battle, clapping his wings.

Lines 701–756

While the battle between Thalestris and Belinda's enemies, the Baron and Clarissa, rages on, Belinda surprises the Baron by pouncing upon him in line 720. Belinda throws some snuff into the Baron's face to confuse him and to make him sneeze. "Now meet thy fate," Belinda yells to the Baron as she draws a "deadly" weapon from her side—a bodkin or ornamental pin. The speaker compares Belinda's pin with Agamemnon's scepter in lines 733–740 in another parody of an epic simile. Belinda demands restoration of the lock. According to the speaker, Belinda is more fierce than Shakespeare's *Othello* when he screamed for the return of Desdemona's handkerchief. However, confusion reigns supreme and no one can locate the lock of hair. After all this fighting and quarreling, the prize has apparently disappeared.

Lines 757–794

Belinda's precious lock of hair cannot be found. Perhaps the lock has gone to the moon "since all things lost on earth are treasured there" (line 758), apparently a popular belief of the time. The moon is also home of heroes' wits, love letters, broken vows, lovers' hearts, courtiers' promises, and other tokens of tender passions. However, the muse of poetry—either John Caryll or Calliope—saw the lock rise towards heaven and become a star. The speaker compares this ascension of the lock to Romulus of Roman mythology, the legendary founder of Rome who was snatched up to heaven in a storm cloud while he was reviewing his army. Thus, the lock will become visible to astronomers and consecrate Belinda's name to eternity. Belinda has at last achieved her desired honor.

Themes

Pride

"The Rape of the Lock" concerns a teenage coquette whose lock of hair is cut off by a suitor. Ordinarily, such an act would be regarded as bizarre, but certainly not as terrible as the "rape" mentioned in the poem's title. However, to the characters of the poem, the ruin of one's hair is like a rape, since their egos are so all consuming that they think of little besides their own appearance.

The poem's protagonist, Belinda, is one of the most vain creations in English literature. A spoiled and beautiful girl, she begins the poem by awaking from a prophetic dream, the important contents of which she forgets because she opens her eyes on a love letter, which appeals to her vanity and thus causes her to dismiss more important matters. Pope's long description of Belinda's readying herself for her trip to Hampton Court likens the application of her makeup to a religious service: the "sacred rites of pride" that Belinda initiates (with the help of her lady-in-waiting, an "inferior priestess") reveal the great attention she pays to her appearance. Once at Hampton Court, Belinda flirts with "well-dressed youths" to draw attention to herself, and her skill in doing so reflects the degree to which she has perfected her coquettish arts:

Her lively looks a sprightly mind

disclose,
Quick as her eyes, and as unfixed as
those:
Favors to none, to all she smiles
extends;
Oft she rejects, but never once
offends.
Bright as the sun, her eyes the gazers
strike,
And, like the sun, they shine on all
alike.

Belinda knows she is beautiful and uses her beauty as a way to satisfy her desire to be noticed and admired.

Belinda, however, is not the poem's only proud person: the baron, who covets Belinda's beauty and aspires to possess her, has an ego to rival that of Belinda. After being defeated in a card game by Belinda—and thus humiliated at such a prominent social gathering—the Baron cuts Belinda's hair (or "rapes her lock") to assert himself after such a devastating defeat. After snipping and seizing the hair that was Belinda's trademark, the baron exalts his power to the sky and bombastically boasts of his strength:

"Let wreaths of triumph now my
temples twine,"
The victor cried, "the glorious prize
is mine!
While fish in streams, or birds
delight in air,
Or in a coach and six the British

Fair,
As long as *Atalantis* shall be read,
Or the small pillow grace a lady's bed,
While visits shall be paid on solemn days,
When numerous wax-lights in bright order blaze,
While nymphs take treats, or assignations give,
So long my honor, name, and praise shall live!"

Topics for Further Study

- Write a short story that shows the foolishness of male or female vanity. Set your story in an imaginary land that you have made up just for this occasion.

- Compare Poepe's poem to Samuel

Taylor Coleridge's *The Rime of the Ancient Mariner,* which is also extremely lengthy. Which poet's style do you think makes reading a long poem easier? Which story is a reader more likely to become absorbed in? Why?

- Do you agree with the roles of the two sexes as shown in Pope's poem? Refer to specific examples in explaining your thoughts.

Like Belinda, the baron is obsessed with his reputation and status—both of which he assumes will skyrocket with his possession of the lock. In a poem where egos as large as these clash, the reader is invited to examine his or her own ego to see if it ever approaches such ridiculous heights.

Beauty

While Belinda is certainly vain, she also possesses an undeniable beauty. Her very name means "beautiful" in Spanish, suggesting that she is the personification of physical attractiveness. Ariel, her guardian sylph, addresses her as "Fairest of mortals" and tells her that a troop of airy spirits hover round her, always on the lookout to address any lapses in beauty that might occur:

> "Our humbler province is to tend the Fair . . .

To save the powder from too rude a gale,
Nor let the imprisoned essences exhale;
To draw fresh colors from the vernal flowers;
To steal from rainbows e'er they drop in showers
A brighter wash; to curl their waving hairs,
Assist their blushes, and inspire their airs;
Nay oft, in dreams invention we bestow,
To change a flounce, or add a furbelow."

Belinda is so "fair" that her invisible army perfects her "powder" and "fresh colors" (makeup), "imprisoned essences" (perfume), and "waving hairs," as well as the ornaments of her dresses ("a flounce" or a "furbelow"). Only the "fairest of mortals" warrants such treatment.

When Belinda arrives at Hampton Court, Pope describes the effects of her beauty on all who see her; calling her "the rival" of the sun, he remarks that "every eye was fixed on her alone." Pope even remarks, "On her white breast a sparkling cross she wore, / Which Jews might kiss, and infidels adore," stressing, in the poem's hyperbolic fashion, the power of Belinda's physical charms. Pope also narrows the reader's focus to Belinda's locks, which epitomize her overall beauty, and its effect on the men who see it:

> Love in these labyrinths his slaves
> detains,
> And mighty hearts are held in
> slender chains.
> With hairy springes we the birds
> betray,
> Slight lines of hair surprise the finny
> prey,
> Fair tresses man's imperial race
> ensnare,
> And beauty draws us with a single
> hair.

Here, Belinda's hair—and, by extension, her beauty—is likened to a trap: as materials like hair are used to catch birds and fish (the "finny prey"), Belinda's hair is so stunning that it "ensnares" all who gaze at it. This, according to the poem, is an unalterable law of nature—a law whose truth is demonstrated in the acts of the baron, who "the bright locks admired" and who "implored / Propitious Heaven" to gain the "prize."

After Belinda's hair is "raped" by the baron, she is naturally upset and laments her newly-marred appearance. However, Pope informs her in the poem's final lines that her lock has become a constellation, forever brightening the night sky like the lock of Bernice, the wife of Ptolemy III whose hair was also enshrined in the stars. The poem's final couplet—"This Lock the Muse shall consecrate to fame, / And 'midst the stars inscribe Belinda's name"—explains that Belinda's beauty will be forever admired, as true beauty has been since people first gazed at the sky. Like the stars themselves, Belinda's beauty is a source of inspiration to all who see her; and it always will be.

Style

"The Rape of the Lock" is the finest example of a mock-epic in English. The poem's 794 lines are divided into five cantos or sections. The word "canto" is derived from the Latin cantus or song; it originally signified a section of a narrative poem sung by a minstrel. "The Rape of the Lock" is written in heroic couplets, lines of iambic pentameter, rhyming aa, bb, cc, and so forth. The description "heroic" was first used in the seventeenth century because of the frequent use of such couplets in epic poems. This couplet style was first used in English by Geoffrey Chaucer in The Canterbury Tales. Pope was the greatest master of the metrical and rhetorical possibilities of the heroic couplet; he turned this concise, restrictive form into a dynamic world of ideas and characters. Pope achieved diversity of style within the couplet by changing the position of the caesura or line break. He expertly balanced the two lines, often using a slight pause at the end of the first line and a heavy stop at the end of the second line. Moreover, he frequently balanced a statement of a thesis and antithesis somewhere within each line, as in these lines from his "Essay on Criticism:"

> Careless of censure, nor too fond of fame; Still pleased to praise, yet not afraid to blame; Averse alike to flatter, or offend; Not free from faults, nor yet too vain to mend.

The caesura moves around within each line, sometimes coming after four syllables and sometimes after seven. Moreover, Pope balances a main idea or thesis within each line with a statement of its opposite or antithesis. He displays great ingenuity and wit in his skillful compression of ideas. The structure of "The Rape of the Lock" roughly corresponds to that of many epics: invocation to a muse (Canto I), conference of the protective gods (Canto II), games and epic banquet (Canto III), the journey into the underworld (Canto IV), and heroic battle and climax (Canto V). Pope both satirizes and honors the elevated style of epic poetry and many of its conventions such as a formal statement of theme, division into cantos, grandiose speeches, challenges, boasts, description of warriors' battle equipment, warfare, epic similes, and supernatural elements. However, the poem ridicules the silly social manners of the aristocracy and deflates the elevated sense of importance in the affairs of wealthy ladies and gentlemen. Yet, the poem also displays some fondness for the grace and beauty of that world. Pope enjoys all the ivory and tortoise shell, cosmetics and diamonds, expensive furniture, silver coffee service, fancy china, and light conversation—this was the world in which he moved attempting to find patronage for his poetry.

Historical Context

The eighteenth century is alternatively known as "The Enlightenment" or "The Age of Reason," two labels indicative of the era and the personality of the time. In the broadest sense, the term *eighteenth-century literature* encompasses writing from the Restoration of Charles II in 1660 to the publication of Wordsworth and Coleridge's collection of Romantic poems, *Lyrical Ballads,* in 1798. Of course, literary periods overlap, and new styles and attitudes do not arrive or disappear as with the flip of a switch. However, one can gain a general understanding of eighteenth-century literary forms and content by examining the ways in which historical events shaped the minds of the writers living through them, as well as reviewing the subjects of some of the era's most notable books.

The seventeenth century saw the outbreak of a terrible civil war, in which Puritan Parliamentary forces clashed with Royalist supporters of King Charles I. Eventually, the Puritans, led by Oliver Cromwell, prevailed, and in 1649 Charles I was tried and beheaded by the victors. A period known as the Interregnum began, where Cromwell led the country as Lord Protector until his death in 1658, when his son, Richard, assumed the title—only to abdicate and set the scene for more national chaos. Eventually, through a series of negotiations, Charles II—the former king's son—was brought out of hiding and returned to London, where the monarchy was restored in 1660. England now yearned for an era of lasting peace, which it mostly enjoyed, although peace was deterred by the outbreak of the bubonic plague in 1665 and the Great Fire of London, which occurred in 1666. Civil unrest and war, therefore, drove the English mind to search for ways in which to establish an ordered understanding of the world, and this search was fueled by the 1662 formation of the Royal Society, an organization of scientists working to share their findings with each other.

As scientists struggled to cultivate a view of the world based on reason rather than superstition, authors of the time likewise sought to explore their world from an intellectual rather than emotional stance. In 1660, John Locke published his *Essay Concerning Human Understanding,* a philosophical work exploring (among other things) the ways in which the five senses apprehend the world and thereby form one's mind. The year 1726 saw the publication of Jonathan Swift's *Gulliver's Travels,* a satiric look at the ways in which mankind abuses his reasonable faculties. In 1755, Samuel Johnson completed what could be called the most representative eighteenth-century work: his *Dictionary of the English Language.* This first, exhaustive English dictionary reflects the Enlightenment desire for order, for a dictionary's primary purpose is to fix the language at a given point in time. Even recreation was viewed as an orderly activity, as seen in the publication in 1760 of Hoyle's *Rules for Whist and Other Popular Card Games.* Other notable monuments to reason published in this era include the first edition of the *Encyclopedia Britannica* (1768), Goldsmith's *History of the Earth and Animated Nature* (1774), Burke's *Reflections of the Revolution in France* (1760), and Gibbon's *Decline and Fall of the Roman Empire* (1776).

Part of the era's love of reason manifested itself in a renewed interest in heralded classical authors, resulting in the era sometimes being called the Neoclassical Age. Homer's *Iliad* (composed circa 750–650 B.C.) was viewed as the pinnacle of poetry, and when Pope began his translation of this epic in 1715 (completed in 1720), he guaranteed himself financial stability. Because of the great number of readers familiar with Homer's epic, Pope was able to parody it in both "The Rape of the Lock" (1714) and "The Dunciad" (1728). Like many poets of his day, Pope felt that his work, in part, should illuminate the tendencies of humanity as a whole; in this sense, art was thought to be a kind of science, which examined the world as intensely as the Royal Society. Pope's satiric style, keen wit, lofty diction, and strict meter are all qualities associated with Enlightenment poets; his stature as a public figure—rather than a solitary, "tortured" artist—is also indicative of the way writers were perceived by the reading public. However, the publication (and success of) Wordsworth and Coleridge's *Lyrical Ballads* in 1798 took poetry in a new direction, away from the reason-based literature of the Enlightenment and into the emotionally charged Romantic era.

Compare & Contrast

- **1687:** Sir Isaac Newton publishes his *Philosophiae Naturalis Principia Mathematica (The Mathematical Principles of Natural Philosophy),* the revolutionary book containing his work on gravity. The book marks the Enlightenment as a time of great scientific progress.

  1859: Charles Darwin publishes his *Origin of Species,* the work containing his theory of natural selection.

  1921: Albert Einstein publishes *The Meaning of Relativity* in which he explores the workings of the space-time continuum. His mathematical formula for relativity is added to the book in 1950.

- **1755:** Samuel Johnson finishes his monumental *Dictionary of the English Language,* printed in two large folio volumes.

  1884: The *Oxford English Dictionary,* containing the history of every word in the English language, begins publication, which will be complete in 1928.

  1986: The final supplement to the

Oxford English Dictionary is published.

Today: The *Oxford English Dictionary* is available on CD-ROM.

- **1720:** Pope publishes the final books of his translation of Homer's *Iliad,* which proves to be very successful. His translation is written in rhyming (or "heroic") couplets of iambic pentameter.

  1990: After a period of years in which the general reading public's interest in Homer has declined, Robert Fagles, a professor at Princeton University, publishes his translation of the *Iliad* to rave reviews and surprisingly high sales. Fagles' translation is written in a looser meter than Pope's.

Critical Overview

The criticism on a major author like Alexander Pope is so rich that a brief survey cannot adequately account for the diversity and breadth of analysis. However, the following three critics (one each from the eighteenth, nineteenth, and twentieth centuries) agree on Pope's enormous achievement. Samuel Johnson, one of Pope's contemporaries, writes in "Pope" in his *Lives of the English Poets* that "The Rape of the Lock" is "the most attractive of all ludicrous compositions," in which "new things are made familiar, and familiar things made new." According to Johnson, "The Rape of the Lock" exhibits to a high degree the two most engaging powers of an author. Johnson says Pope creates a race of imaginary creatures never witnessed before and presents them in a style in perfect accord with his purpose. Although Johnson says the poem's subject is "below the common incidents in common life," he praises Pope's wit and imagination in carrying off such an excellently silly composition. William Hazlitt wrote in "On Dryden and Pope" in his *Lectures on the English Poets and the English Comic Writers* that he considered "The Rape of the Lock" to be "the most exquisite specimen of filigree work ever invented." Hazlitt praises Pope's ability to lend a decorous beauty to every element in the poem from characters to props to dialogue and description. Hazlitt writes that "a toilette is described with the solemnity of an altar raised to the

Goddess of Vanity, and the history of a silver bodkin [a pin] is given with all the pomp of heraldry." According to Hazlitt, the true achievement of the poem is its ability to balance concealed irony and apparent seriousness. Great things are made trivial and trivial things elevated to ridiculous heights, leaving the reader dazzled and uncertain as to whether he or she should laugh or cry. A more recent evaluation by Stanley Edgar Hyman in "English Romanticism" in *Poetry and Criticism: Four Revolutions in Literary Taste* demonstrates several ways of interpreting "The Rape of the Lock." In general, Hyman says it would be a mistake to look for hidden political messages, Marxist yearning for revolution, or mythological renderings of Belinda as the corn maiden "raped" by the Baron in a fertility ritual. However, Hyman goes on to find exactly these types of hidden meanings in the poem because it is so rich and allusive. Hyman believes that perhaps critics have been too easygoing in their reading of the poem, not finding the hidden messages that Pope carefully left behind. Perhaps most appealing to Hyman are the hidden sexual messages: "The poem is one vast comic symbolic defloration. . . . 'Lock' is a pun on Freud's lock that all keys fit. . . . Its rape by the baron is a sex act." Hyman also finds ample evidence for political and mythological interpretive possibilities. "The Rape of the Lock" seems capable of supporting many different kinds of readings.

What Do I Read Next?

- Pope's "An Essay on Criticism" (1711) is a long poem in which he prescribes his rules for good poetry and attacks a number of poetic clichés.

- Like "The Rape of the Lock," Pope's "An Epistle to Dr. Arbuthnot" (1735) is a satirical work; this time, Pope's targets are the amateur poets who constantly seek his approval.

- One of Pope's four *Moral Essays* (1735) is subtitled "Of the Characters of Women;" this poem is an interesting companion piece to "The Rape of the Lock" in the ways that it treats what Pope saw as the concerns and personalities of women.

- Jonathan Swift's poem "The Progress of Beauty" (1719), like "The Rape of the Lock," examines the ways in which cosmetics altar a woman's appearance.

- The American novelist Henry James' second novel, *Roderick Hudson* (1875), concerns a sculptor who, like Pope's baron, is haunted by the beauty of a striking woman.

- Samuel Johnson's series of essays known as *The Rambler* addresses a number of topics; his "Rambler 155" (1751) examines the ways in which one's own vanity prevents him or her from taking advice. This is a good essay to read after considering Clarissa's speech about "good sense."

Sources

Brower, Reuben A., "Am'rous Causes," reprinted in *Twentieth Century Interpretations of "The Rape of the Lock,"* edited by G. S. Rousseau, Prentice-Hall, 1969, pp. 52–68.

Grove, Robin, *The Art of Alexander Pope,* excerpt reprinted in *Alexander Pope's "The Rape of the Lock,"* edited by Harold Bloom, Chelsea House, 1988, pp. 33–65.

Hazlitt, William, "On Dryden and Pope," in *Lectures on the English Poets and the English Comic Writers,* edited by William Carew Hazlitt, George Bell and Sons, 1894, pp. 91–113.

Hyman, Stanley Edgar, "English Romanticism," in *Poetry and Criticism: Four Revolutions in Literary Taste,* Athenaeum, 1961, pp. 85–128.

Johnson, Samuel, "Pope," in *Lives of the English Poets,* Vol. II, Oxford University Press, 1967, pp. 223–344.

Pope, Alexander, "Essay on Criticism," in *English Critical Essays,* edited by Edmund D. Jones, Oxford University Press, 1922.

———, *The Poems of Alexander Pope,* Yale University Press, 1993.

Rumbold, Valerie, *Women's Place in Pope's World,* Cambridge University Press, 1989, p. 80.

Trimble, John, "Clarissa's Role in 'The Rape of the

Lock,'" in *Texas Studies in English,* Vol. 15, 1974, pp. 673–691.

Williams, Aubrey, "The 'Fall' of China and 'The Rape of the Lock,'" reprinted in *The Rape of the Lock,* edited by David G. Lougee and Robert W. McHenry Jr., Merrill, 1969, pp. 119–128.

For Further Study

Bernard, John, ed., *Pope: The Critical Heritage,* Routlage & Kegan Paul, 1973.

> This collection features original reviews of Pope's work when it first appeared. It provides some of the very first reactions to "The Rape of the Lock."

Johnson, Samuel, *Rasselas, Poems, and Selected Prose,* Holt, Rinehart and Winston, 1952.

> This anthology of Johnson's writing features his entire *Life of Pope,* which was published in 1781, thirty–seven years after Pope's death.

Mack, Maynard, *Alexander Pope: A Life,* W. W. Norton & Company, 1986.

> Mack's text is an exhaustive and definitive biography of Pope that illuminates his poetry as well as his times.

Rousseau, G. S., ed., *Twentieth Century Interpretations of "The Rape of the Lock,"* Prentice-Hall, 1969.

> These collected critical essays feature examinations of the poem's mock-heroic elements as well as a section of shorter critical passages.

Tillotson, Geoffrey, ed., *Eighteenth Century English Literature,* Harcourt Brace Jovanovich, 1969.

> This brilliantly edited anthology features extensive selections by Pope, copious notes to the allusions in his poems, and a short but comprehensive introductory essay on Enlightenment literature as a whole. This is a valuable source for the student who wants to learn about the literary climate of Pope's day.